Artificial intelligence Powered
Turbines

The AI Turbine Handbook:

A Comprehensive Guide to Optimizing Operations, Troubleshooting, and Maintenance in Power Generation

JAMES BRANDY

TABLE OF CONTENTS

INTRODUCTION

As the energy landscape undergoes a transformative shift towards sustainability and efficiency, the integration of Artificial Intelligence (AI) stands at the forefront of revolutionizing power generation. In this comprehensive guide, "The AI Turbine Handbook," we embark on a journey into the intricate nexus of AI and turbine operations, unraveling the profound impact of intelligent technologies on the efficiency, reliability, and sustainability of power generation.

The chapters ahead delve into the core principles of AI and its strategic application within the intricate machinery of power generation turbines. As we explore the intricacies of AI integration, the objective is not only to optimize operational processes but also to elevate turbine performance to unprecedented levels. We will unravel the significance of AI in transforming traditional turbine operations into dynamic, data-driven systems capable of adapting in real time to varying demands and conditions.

Understanding the symbiosis between AI and turbine operations is paramount as we navigate the complexities of this synergy. From harnessing predictive maintenance strategies to unleashing the power of machine learning for performance enhancement, each facet of AI's role in turbine operations is meticulously examined. Through practical insights, case studies, and forward-thinking analysis, this book aims to equip professionals, researchers, and enthusiasts alike with the knowledge needed to harness the full potential of AI in the dynamic realm of power generation.

Join us on this enlightening expedition as we unravel the layers of innovation, uncover the challenges, and chart the course for a future where AI not only powers turbines but propels the entire energy industry into a new era of efficiency, sustainability, and operational excellence.

CHAPTER ONE
Introduction to Power Generation Turbines

In the opening chapter of our exploration into the Fundamentals of Turbine Technology, we embark on a journey to unravel the core principles that drive the heart of power generation. Turbines, the workhorses of energy conversion, play a pivotal role in transforming various energy sources into electricity. This chapter lays the groundwork for a comprehensive understanding of these dynamic machines.

1.1 Basics of Power Generation Turbines:

We begin by delving into the fundamental types of turbines that shape the landscape of power generation. Whether harnessing the power of steam, gas, or water, turbines exhibit diverse configurations, each tailored to extract energy efficiently. Through a comparative exploration, we unveil the distinctive characteristics and applications of steam turbines, gas turbines, and hydro turbines.

1.2 Working Principles:

Understanding the essence of turbine operation is crucial to appreciating their role in energy conversion. This section unravels the thermodynamic principles that govern the transformation of potential energy into mechanical energy and, subsequently, into electrical power. The chapter elucidates the intricacies of how turbines serve as conduits for this energy transformation, laying the groundwork for subsequent discussions on optimization and enhancement.

1.3 Key Components of Turbines:

Turbines are intricate machines comprised of various components that harmonize to facilitate energy conversion. Readers will gain insights into the essential elements such as rotors and stators, as well as the significance of blades and vanes in extracting energy effectively. The chapter not only outlines the physical components but also elucidates their functional roles within the broader turbine system.

1.4 Turbine Systems:

To maintain operational control and ensure longevity, turbines rely on sophisticated governing, lubrication, and cooling systems. This section navigates through the intricacies of these systems, highlighting their importance in regulating turbine speed, minimizing friction, and managing thermal stresses. A comprehensive understanding of these systems forms the foundation for discussions on advanced control mechanisms and intelligent interventions in subsequent chapters.

1.5 Conclusion:

Chapter 1 concludes by emphasizing the pivotal role of turbines in the power generation landscape and setting the stage for a deeper exploration into the synergy between traditional turbine technology and the innovative applications of Artificial Intelligence. As we delve further into the book, the fundamentals established in this chapter will serve as a compass, guiding readers through the intricate pathways of turbine operations and the intelligent solutions that enhance their performance.

CHAPTER TWO

AI Integration in Turbine Operations

In the dynamic landscape of power generation, Chapter 2 unfolds the transformative role of Artificial Intelligence (AI) in enhancing the efficiency of turbine operations. As we delve into "The AI Turbine Handbook," this chapter illuminates the intelligent interventions that redefine how turbines operate, introducing a paradigm shift towards optimization, real-time adaptability, and heightened performance.

2.1 Incorporating AI for Enhanced Efficiency:

This section explores the strategic integration of AI into traditional turbine operations, unveiling how machine intelligence augments and amplifies efficiency. Readers will gain insights into the ways AI optimizes processes, from energy extraction to power generation, resulting in enhanced overall turbine performance. Case studies and success stories underscore the tangible benefits derived from incorporating AI for efficiency gains.

2.2 Real-time Monitoring:

AI's prowess becomes particularly evident in its ability to enable real-time monitoring of turbine operations. We delve into advanced sensors, data acquisition systems, and IoT technologies that provide a continuous stream of operational data. The chapter elucidates how AI processes this influx of information instantaneously, empowering operators with unprecedented insights into turbine health, performance metrics, and potential issues.

2.3 Adaptive Controls:

The concept of adaptive controls takes center stage as we explore how AI empowers turbines to dynamically respond to changing conditions. This section dissects the intricacies of adaptive control algorithms that enable turbines to adjust parameters in real time, optimizing performance under varying loads, temperatures, and other dynamic factors. The chapter showcases how adaptive controls enhance operational flexibility and responsiveness.

2.4 AI-Enhanced Decision Making:

AI not only monitors and adapts but also contributes to intelligent decision-making processes within turbine operations. This part of the chapter sheds light on how AI algorithms analyze vast datasets to predict potential issues, recommend maintenance schedules, and optimize operational parameters. The result is a shift from reactive to proactive decision-making, minimizing downtime and maximizing efficiency.

2.5 Ensuring Reliability through AI:

Reliability is paramount in power generation, and AI plays a crucial role in ensuring the consistent and dependable operation of turbines. This section explores how AI-driven predictive analytics, failure prediction models, and preventive maintenance strategies contribute to the overall reliability of turbine systems.

Chapter 2 establishes a foundation for understanding how AI seamlessly integrates into turbine operations, elevating efficiency, providing real-time insights, and fostering adaptive controls that respond dynamically to the ever-changing demands of the power generation landscape. As we navigate through subsequent chapters, the symbiotic relationship between AI and turbines unfolds, shaping the future of energy generation.

CHAPTER THREE

Troubleshooting with AI

In the pursuit of operational excellence, Chapter 3 of "The AI Turbine Handbook" delves into the realm of troubleshooting, uncovering the transformative role of Artificial Intelligence (AI) in diagnosing and addressing common turbine issues. This chapter illuminates the sophisticated methodologies and intelligent algorithms that empower turbines to not only identify potential faults but also proactively mitigate them.

3.1 AI-Based Diagnostics and Fault Detection:

This section unravels the intricacies of AI-based diagnostics, where machine learning algorithms and advanced data analytics become powerful tools for identifying potential issues within turbine systems. Readers will gain insights into the development and deployment of fault detection models, examining how AI can analyze operational data to detect anomalies and pre-emptively diagnose impending problems.

3.2 Addressing Common Turbine Issues:

Building upon the diagnostic capabilities of AI, this part of the chapter explores how intelligent technologies are applied to address a spectrum of common turbine issues. From vibration analysis to temperature variations and pressure fluctuations, AI-driven systems showcase their ability to not only pinpoint the root causes but also recommend targeted solutions. Case studies highlight instances where AI has played a pivotal role in resolving complex turbine challenges.

3.3 Proactive Maintenance Strategies:

The integration of AI in troubleshooting extends beyond mere fault detection; it lays the foundation for proactive maintenance strategies. This section navigates through the landscape of predictive maintenance, where AI algorithms analyze historical data, predict potential failures, and recommend maintenance actions. The result is a shift from reactive to preventative measures, minimizing downtime and optimizing turbine longevity.

3.4 Intelligent Alarm Systems:

AI revolutionizes the conventional alarm systems within turbine operations. We explore how AI enhances alarm accuracy, reducing false positives and negatives. Intelligent alarm systems not only identify issues but also prioritize them based on severity and potential impact, allowing operators to focus their attention on critical matters and streamline the troubleshooting process.

3.5 Human-AI Collaboration in Troubleshooting:

Acknowledging the synergy between human expertise and AI capabilities, this section emphasizes the importance of collaborative troubleshooting. AI serves as a valuable assistant, augmenting human decision-making processes with data-driven insights. Case studies showcase successful collaborations where operators and AI work hand-in-hand to swiftly and accurately troubleshoot turbine issues.

Chapter 3 unveils the power of AI in troubleshooting, showcasing how intelligent diagnostics, fault detection, and proactive maintenance strategies redefine the approach to common turbine issues. As we navigate through the subsequent chapters, the integration of AI as a troubleshooting ally continues to unfold, shaping a future where turbine operations are not just efficient but also resilient in the face of challenges.

CHAPTER FOUR

Maintenance Strategies with AI

As we delve deeper into "The AI Turbine Handbook," Chapter 4 unravels the symbiotic relationship between Artificial Intelligence (AI) and maintenance strategies, illuminating how predictive techniques and proactive measures contribute to the longevity and optimal performance of power generation turbines.

4.1 Predictive Maintenance Techniques:

This section explores how AI transforms the traditional approach to maintenance through predictive techniques. AI algorithms analyze historical operational data, identifying patterns and trends that enable the anticipation of potential failures. By predicting when specific components might require attention, predictive maintenance minimizes downtime, optimizes resource allocation, and extends the overall lifespan of turbines.

4.2 Proactive Measures for Turbine Longevity:

Proactivity is at the heart of this chapter as we delve into how AI enables operators to take strategic measures to ensure the longevity of turbines. From monitoring wear and tear on critical components to adjusting operational parameters based on AI-driven insights, proactive measures become integral in mitigating potential issues before they escalate. Real-world examples highlight instances where proactive interventions have significantly enhanced turbine durability.

4.3 Condition-Based Maintenance:

AI's role in condition-based maintenance is examined, showcasing how continuous monitoring and analysis of turbine conditions guide maintenance decisions. This section delves into how AI-driven systems assess the health of various components, enabling operators to schedule maintenance activities based on the actual condition of the turbine rather than predetermined schedules. The result is a more efficient and targeted approach to maintaining turbine health.

4.4 Optimization of Maintenance Resources:

Efficient resource allocation is a key benefit of AI-driven maintenance strategies. The chapter explores how AI assists in optimizing the allocation of maintenance resources by prioritizing tasks based on criticality and predicting the optimal times for intervention. This proactive resource management ensures that maintenance efforts are focused where they are most needed, minimizing costs and maximizing effectiveness.

4.5 Integration of AI with Existing Maintenance Practices:

Recognizing the need for a seamless transition, this section discusses strategies for integrating AI with existing maintenance practices. By leveraging AI as a complementary tool within established maintenance frameworks, operators can harness the benefits of advanced technologies without disrupting established workflows. Case studies demonstrate successful integrations that have streamlined maintenance operations.

Chapter 4 sets the stage for a paradigm shift in turbine maintenance, where AI-driven predictive techniques and proactive measures become instrumental in ensuring the longevity and sustained efficiency of power generation turbines. As we progress through the subsequent chapters, the focus on maintenance strategies with AI continues to evolve, shaping a landscape where turbines are not just maintained but optimized for enduring performance.

Recognizing the need for a seamless transition, this section discusses strategies for integrating AI with existing maintenance practices. By leveraging AI as a complementary tool within established maintenance frameworks, operators can harness the benefits of advanced technologies without disrupting established workflows. Case studies demonstrate successful integrations that have streamlined maintenance operations.

Chapter 4 sets the stage for a paradigm shift in turbine maintenance, where AI-driven predictive techniques and proactive measures become instrumental in ensuring the longevity and sustained efficiency of power generation turbines. As we progress through the subsequent chapters, the focus on maintenance strategies with AI continues to evolve, shaping a landscape where turbines are not just maintained but optimized for enduring performance.

CHAPTER FIVE

Data Analytics for Turbine Optimization

In the ongoing exploration of "The AI Turbine Handbook," Chapter 5 delves into the critical role of data analytics in optimizing turbine performance. This chapter unveils how the strategic leverage of data, coupled with advanced analytics, becomes a cornerstone in the pursuit of enhanced efficiency and informed decision-making within power generation turbines.

5.1 Leveraging Data for Improved Performance:

This section opens by elucidating the wealth of data generated by turbines during their operational lifespan. Readers gain insights into the types of data collected, spanning from operational parameters and sensor readings to historical performance metrics. The chapter explores how this data becomes a valuable resource for understanding turbine behavior and lays the groundwork for subsequent analytics-driven optimizations.

5.2 Analytics-driven Decision Making:

Transitioning from data collection to actionable insights, this part of the chapter delves into the application of analytics for informed decision-making. AI-driven algorithms analyze vast datasets to identify patterns, correlations, and anomalies. The result is a decision-making process informed by predictive analytics, enabling operators to make strategic choices that enhance turbine performance, minimize downtime, and optimize energy production.

5.3 Performance Metrics and Key Indicators:

Understanding turbine performance requires the definition and analysis of key metrics. This section explores the development and utilization of performance indicators that serve as benchmarks for optimization efforts. From efficiency metrics to reliability indices, the chapter demonstrates how analytics contribute to establishing and continuously refining these crucial performance benchmarks.

5.4 Continuous Monitoring and Feedback Loops:

The concept of continuous monitoring takes center stage as we explore how analytics establish real-time feedback loops. By continuously analyzing operational data, AI-driven systems provide instant feedback on turbine performance. This iterative process enables operators to make rapid adjustments, fine-tuning operational parameters for optimal efficiency and responsiveness.

5.5 Predictive Analytics for Future Optimization:

Predictive analytics extends beyond immediate decision-making, shaping the future of turbine optimization. This section navigates through how AI models forecast trends, potential issues, and opportunities for improvement. By predicting future scenarios, operators can proactively implement changes, ensuring that turbines are not just optimized for the present but are resilient and adaptive to evolving operational demands.

Chapter 5 sheds light on the transformative power of data analytics in optimizing turbine performance. From leveraging data for improved insights to analytics-driven decision-making, this chapter sets the stage for a data-centric approach that not only enhances current turbine operations but paves the way for future advancements. As we progress through the subsequent chapters, the focus on data

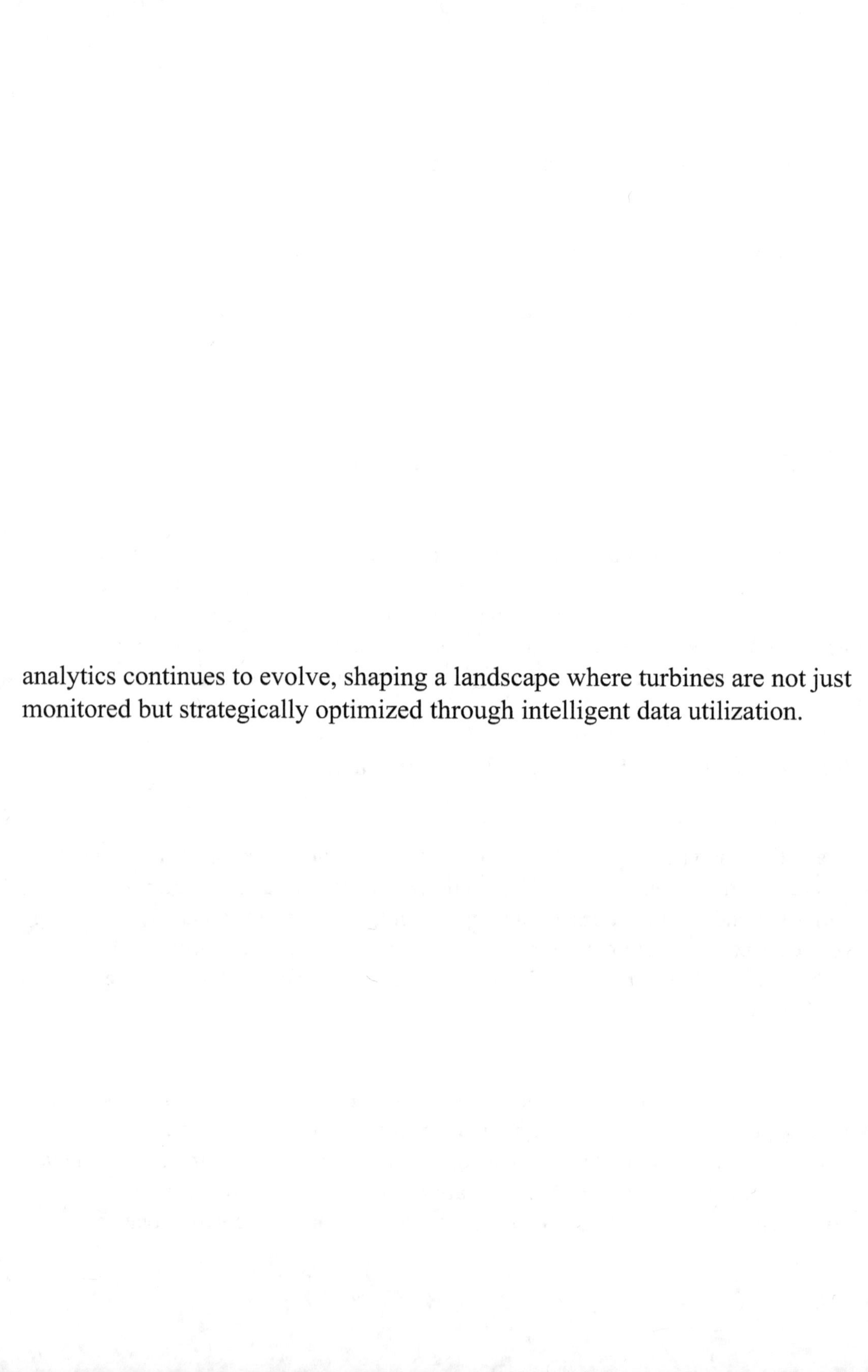

analytics continues to evolve, shaping a landscape where turbines are not just monitored but strategically optimized through intelligent data utilization.

CHAPTER SIX

Machine Learning Applications

As we delve deeper into the intersection of Artificial Intelligence and turbine operations in "The AI Turbine Handbook," Chapter 6 explores the transformative applications of Machine Learning (ML). Focused on performance prediction and drawing insights from historical data, this chapter unveils how ML algorithms become pivotal in anticipating and optimizing the behavior of power generation turbines.

6.1 ML Algorithms for Turbine Performance Prediction:

This section introduces readers to the diverse range of ML algorithms tailored for predicting turbine performance. From regression models to more sophisticated ensemble methods, the chapter explores how these algorithms analyze various parameters, historical performance data, and external factors to forecast turbine behavior. Case studies highlight instances where ML predictions have been instrumental in optimizing operational parameters for enhanced efficiency.

6.2 Learning from Historical Data:

Delving into the heart of machine learning applications, this part of the chapter emphasizes the importance of historical data as a training ground for ML algorithms. By examining past operational patterns, failures, and successes, ML models learn to discern correlations and trends, enabling them to make accurate predictions about future turbine behavior. The repetitious learning process ensures continuous improvement and adaptability.

6.3 Feature Selection and Model Optimization:

The chapter navigates through the critical aspects of feature selection and model optimization in the context of ML applications for turbine performance. Understanding which parameters contribute most to accurate predictions and fine-tuning models to enhance their predictive capabilities become integral components in achieving optimal outcomes. Practical insights shed light on effective strategies for selecting features and optimizing ML models.

6.4 Ensemble Learning for Robust Predictions:

Ensemble learning, a powerful technique in machine learning, takes the spotlight as we explore how combining multiple models enhances prediction robustness. This section provides an overview of ensemble methods such as Random Forests and Gradient Boosting, showcasing how they mitigate individual model biases and contribute to more accurate and reliable predictions in turbine performance.

6.5 Case Studies in ML-Driven Optimization:

The chapter concludes with a series of case studies that illustrate the real-world applications of ML in predicting turbine performance. Readers gain valuable insights into how organizations have successfully implemented ML algorithms to forecast operational parameters, identify potential issues, and optimize turbine efficiency. These case studies serve as practical examples of the tangible benefits derived from embracing machine learning in turbine operations.

Chapter 6 unfolds the realm of machine learning applications, illuminating how predictive algorithms and insights drawn from historical data revolutionize the landscape of turbine performance optimization. As we advance through subsequent chapters, the integration of machine learning continues to shape the narrative of

AI-driven turbine operations, ushering in an era of heightened predictability and efficiency.

CHAPTER SEVEN

Advanced Control Systems

In the evolution of turbine operations, Chapter 7 of "The AI Turbine Handbook" delves into the intricate world of Advanced Control Systems, specifically focusing on how Artificial Intelligence (AI) enhances control mechanisms to optimize turbine response. This chapter unravels the synergies between intelligent technologies and control strategies, paving the way for unprecedented levels of responsiveness and operational precision.

7.1 AI-Enhanced Control Mechanisms:

This section opens by exploring the infusion of AI into traditional control systems, transforming them into intelligent mechanisms capable of adapting to dynamic operational conditions. Readers will gain insights into the integration of machine learning algorithms, neural networks, and adaptive control strategies that augment the responsiveness and adaptability of turbine control mechanisms. Case studies showcase instances where AI-driven control mechanisms have demonstrated superior performance in real-world applications.

7.2 Turbine Response Optimization:

The heart of this chapter lies in understanding how AI contributes to the optimization of turbine response. We delve into the intricacies of response time, stability, and precision, showcasing how AI-driven control mechanisms continuously analyze operational data to adjust parameters in real time. The result is a turbine that responds dynamically to load fluctuations, disturbances, and external factors, achieving optimal performance under varying conditions.

7.3 Adaptive Control Algorithms:

The chapter explores the realm of adaptive control algorithms, highlighting how AI enables turbines to autonomously adjust their control strategies based on learned patterns and evolving operational demands. We delve into the principles of model-based and model-free adaptive control, demonstrating their application in optimizing turbine response and ensuring stability in the face of uncertainties.

7.4 Learning from Operational Data:

Understanding the significance of learning from operational data, this section emphasizes the continuous learning loop embedded within AI-enhanced control systems. By analyzing historical data and real-time feedback, the control mechanisms adapt and evolve, learning from past experiences to enhance future responses. The iterative learning process ensures that turbines not only optimize responses based on current conditions but also improve their adaptability over time.

7.5 Integration Challenges and Solutions:

Acknowledging the challenges in integrating advanced control systems, this part of the chapter discusses common hurdles and effective solutions. From compatibility issues to the need for robust cybersecurity measures, the chapter provides practical insights into successfully integrating AI-enhanced control mechanisms into existing turbine systems. Case studies highlight instances where integration challenges were overcome, leading to significant improvements in operational efficiency.

Chapter 7 unfolds the dynamic landscape of advanced control systems, showcasing how AI-enhanced mechanisms revolutionize turbine response optimization. As we progress through the subsequent chapters, the focus on control systems continues to evolve, shaping a future where turbines not only respond to operational demands but do so with a level of intelligence and adaptability that ensures optimal performance in any scenario.

CHAPTER EIGHT

Cybersecurity in AI-Powered Turbines

In the digital era of power generation, Chapter 8 of "The AI Turbine Handbook" navigates through the critical domain of cybersecurity, focusing on safeguarding turbine systems from evolving cyber threats. This chapter unveils the intricate strategies and best practices that form the foundation for securing AI-powered turbines, ensuring the resilience and reliability of these intelligent systems in the face of cybersecurity challenges.

8.1 Safeguarding Turbine Systems from Cyber Threats:

The chapter commences by examining the landscape of cyber threats that pose risks to AI-powered turbines. From malicious attacks targeting control systems to vulnerabilities within interconnected networks, readers gain insights into the diverse range of cyber threats that turbines may encounter. Understanding these threats lays the groundwork for developing robust cybersecurity measures.

8.2 Importance of Cybersecurity in AI Integration:

Building on the understanding of threats, this section emphasizes the critical role of cybersecurity in the context of AI integration. AI-powered turbines, with their interconnected sensors and data-driven decision-making processes, become potential targets for cyber adversaries. The chapter explores how cybersecurity is not merely a protective layer but an integral component of ensuring the safe and reliable operation of AI-enhanced turbine systems.

8.3 Cybersecurity Best Practices:

A comprehensive overview of best practices forms the core of this chapter. Readers will be introduced to a set of proactive measures and strategies, including encryption protocols, access controls, and intrusion detection systems. The chapter also delves into the importance of regular cybersecurity audits, vulnerability assessments, and continuous monitoring to identify and mitigate potential threats before they can impact turbine operations.

8.4 Securing AI Models and Data:

The unique challenges posed by securing AI models and the vast amounts of data they rely on are explored in this section. From ensuring the integrity of training data to implementing secure storage and transmission of AI-generated insights, the chapter provides insights into safeguarding the core elements of AI integration within turbine systems.

8.5 Training and Awareness Programs:

Recognizing that cybersecurity is a shared responsibility, this part of the chapter focuses on the importance of training and awareness programs. Ensuring that operators, maintenance personnel, and all stakeholders are well-versed in cybersecurity best practices fosters a culture of vigilance and preparedness, minimizing the likelihood of human-related vulnerabilities.

Chapter 8 concludes by underscoring the ever-evolving nature of cybersecurity challenges and the need for a proactive and adaptive approach. As we traverse the subsequent chapters, the theme of cybersecurity remains integral, shaping a future where AI-powered turbines not only operate with intelligence and efficiency but also with resilience against emerging cyber threats.

CHAPTER NINE

Regulatory Compliance

In the intricate landscape of power generation, Chapter 9 of "The AI Turbine Handbook" delves into the crucial domain of regulatory compliance, specifically exploring how Artificial Intelligence (AI) aligns with and supports meeting industry standards. This chapter unravels the complexities of compliance challenges and presents innovative solutions to ensure that AI-powered turbines adhere to the stringent regulatory frameworks governing the energy sector.

9.1 Meeting Industry Standards with AI:

The chapter begins by elucidating the prevailing industry standards and regulations governing power generation. Readers will gain insights into the diverse regulatory landscape, encompassing safety protocols, environmental regulations, and performance standards. As AI becomes an integral component of turbine operations, understanding how it aligns with and contributes to meeting these standards forms the foundation for the subsequent discussions.

9.2 Compliance Challenges in AI Integration:

This section explores the unique challenges posed by integrating AI into the highly regulated field of power generation. From ensuring transparency in AI decision-making to addressing concerns related to data privacy and security, the chapter dissects the compliance challenges that arise as AI becomes a central element in turbine systems. Case studies shed light on instances where regulatory compliance became a focal point in AI integration.

9.3 AI as a Tool for Regulatory Compliance:

Building on the challenges, the chapter delves into the role of AI as a tool for ensuring and enhancing regulatory compliance. AI's ability to analyze vast datasets, predict potential issues, and optimize operational parameters becomes instrumental in proactively meeting and exceeding industry standards. The section explores how AI-driven systems contribute to the development of comprehensive compliance strategies.

9.4 Real-time Monitoring for Compliance Assurance:

One of the key advantages of AI in regulatory compliance is its capability for real-time monitoring. This part of the chapter navigates through how AI-driven monitoring systems provide continuous insights into turbine operations, ensuring that compliance parameters are met instantaneously. The integration of AI into monitoring practices becomes a proactive strategy for compliance assurance.

9.5 Collaborative Approaches to Compliance:

Acknowledging the multifaceted nature of compliance, this section emphasizes the importance of collaborative approaches. The chapter explores how stakeholders, including regulators, industry bodies, and technology developers, can collaborate to establish standards that align with technological advancements. Collaborative initiatives become essential in fostering an environment where AI and regulatory compliance coexist harmoniously.

Chapter 9 concludes by underscoring the pivotal role of regulatory compliance in the deployment of AI-powered turbines. As we progress through the subsequent chapters, the theme of compliance remains integral, shaping a future where AI not only enhances operational efficiency but also operates within the ethical and regulatory frameworks that define the energy sector.

CHAPTER TEN

Case Studies: Successful Implementations of AI in Power Generation

In this pivotal chapter of "The AI Turbine Handbook," we turn our attention to real-world examples and case studies that illuminate the transformative impact of Artificial Intelligence (AI) in power generation. By delving into successful implementations, this chapter provides valuable insights, lessons learned, and practical applications that showcase the power of AI in optimizing turbine operations.

10.1 Enhancing Efficiency with Predictive Maintenance:

The chapter opens with a case study highlighting the implementation of predictive maintenance strategies powered by AI in a power generation facility. By leveraging machine learning algorithms to analyze historical data and identify patterns, the facility achieved a significant reduction in unplanned downtime and maintenance costs, showcasing the tangible benefits of proactive maintenance.

10.2 Dynamic Control Systems in Action:

This section explores a case study where AI-enhanced control systems were implemented to optimize turbine response in real time. The study illustrates how adaptive control algorithms, driven by machine learning, dynamically adjust operational parameters to ensure optimal performance under varying conditions. The outcomes underscore the responsiveness and adaptability gained through the integration of AI into control mechanisms.\

10.3 Cybersecurity Resilience in Turbine Operations:

The chapter delves into a case study highlighting a successful cybersecurity implementation in an AI-powered turbine system. By adopting robust cybersecurity measures, including encryption protocols and continuous monitoring, the facility fortified its turbines against cyber threats, ensuring the safe and secure operation of AI-enhanced systems.

10.4 Data Analytics for Improved Performance:

A case study in this section showcases the strategic application of data analytics in improving turbine performance. By harnessing the power of AI-driven analytics, the facility gained actionable insights into operational patterns, leading to optimized turbine behavior, increased efficiency, and reduced operational costs.

10.5 Regulatory Compliance through AI Integration:

The chapter explores a case study focusing on how AI integration supported a power generation facility in meeting and exceeding regulatory compliance standards. By leveraging AI for real-time monitoring, data analysis, and decision-making, the facility not only adhered to industry regulations but also achieved operational excellence within the stipulated guidelines.

10.6 Human-AI Collaboration for Troubleshooting:

This section features a case study illustrating the successful collaboration between human operators and AI in troubleshooting turbine issues. By combining human expertise with AI-driven diagnostics, the facility streamlined troubleshooting processes, reduced downtime, and enhanced overall operational efficiency.

10.7 Economic Impact of AI in Power Generation:

The chapter concludes with a case study exploring the broader economic impact of AI implementation in power generation. By analyzing cost savings, increased energy output, and improved operational efficiency, this study highlights the economic benefits that arise from successful AI integration in turbine operations.

Chapter 10 encapsulates the practical applications of AI in power generation through a series of diverse case studies. These real-world examples serve as a testament to the transformative potential of AI, providing readers with valuable insights and lessons that can inform their journey toward AI-powered excellence in turbine operations. As we progress through the subsequent chapters, the emphasis on case studies continues, shaping a narrative that celebrates the success stories and innovations emerging from the fusion of AI and power generation.

CHAPTER ELEVEN

Future Trends: Emerging Technologies in Turbine Operations

In this forward-looking chapter of "The AI Turbine Handbook," we explore the horizon of emerging technologies that hold the potential to reshape turbine operations. From innovative advancements in materials science to the continued evolution of Artificial Intelligence (AI), this chapter unveils the future trends that are set to redefine the landscape of power generation.

11.1 Materials Innovations for Turbine Efficiency:

The chapter kicks off by delving into emerging materials science innovations poised to enhance turbine efficiency. From advanced alloys to cutting-edge coatings, we explore how material advancements contribute to increased durability, improved heat resistance, and overall heightened performance in power generation turbines.

11.2 Quantum Computing in Turbine Simulation:

Quantum computing, with its unparalleled computational capabilities, takes center stage in this section. The chapter examines how quantum algorithms are anticipated to revolutionize turbine simulation, enabling complex models and simulations that were once computationally infeasible. Quantum computing holds the promise of accelerating design optimization and refining operational strategies for turbines.

11.3 Internet of Things (IoT) for Enhanced Connectivity:

As the Internet of Things (IoT) continues to mature, we delve into its role in turbine operations. The chapter explores how interconnected sensors and devices contribute to real-time data collection, providing a comprehensive view of turbine performance. The seamless connectivity afforded by IoT paves the way for even more sophisticated AI applications and predictive analytics.

11.4 Edge Computing for Real-Time Decision-Making:

Edge computing emerges as a pivotal technology in this section, focusing on the decentralization of computational processes. By bringing computation closer to the evidence source, edge computing facilitates real-time decision-making within turbine systems. We explore how this trend aligns with the requirements of AI applications, enabling faster response times and reduced latency in critical decision processes.

11.5 Explainable AI for Transparent Decision-Making:

Addressing the importance of transparency in AI decision-making, the chapter discusses the emergence of explainable AI. As AI systems become increasingly complex, the need for understanding the rationale behind decisions becomes crucial. We explore developments in explainable AI that aim to demystify the decision-making processes within power generation turbines.

11.6 AI-Assisted Sustainability Measures:

Sustainability takes precedence in this section, examining how AI can play a pivotal role in enhancing the environmental footprint of power generation. From optimizing energy efficiency to dynamically adjusting operations based on renewable energy availability, the chapter explores AI-driven strategies that contribute to a more sustainable future for turbine operations.

11.7 Autonomous Systems for Turbine Maintenance:

The chapter concludes by envisioning the integration of autonomous systems in turbine maintenance. From robotic inspections to AI-driven maintenance robots, we explore how autonomous technologies are anticipated to streamline maintenance processes, reduce downtime, and enhance overall operational efficiency in power generation turbines.

Chapter 11 provides a glimpse into the exciting future of turbine operations, where emerging technologies converge to shape a landscape of unprecedented efficiency, sustainability, and innovation. As we progress through the subsequent chapters, the focus on future trends continues, providing readers with a roadmap to anticipate and navigate the transformative developments on the horizon of AI-powered turbine operations.

CHAPTER TWELVE

Integration Challenges and Solutions

In this pivotal chapter, we delve into the nuances of overcoming implementation hurdles and establishing best practices for seamless integration of Artificial Intelligence (AI) in turbine operations within "The AI Turbine Handbook."

12.1 Identifying Common Integration Challenges:

The chapter begins by dissecting common challenges encountered during the integration of AI into turbine operations. Challenges encompass data complexities, organizational resistance, and the intricacies of aligning AI with existing infrastructure. By identifying these hurdles, organizations can tailor solutions to their specific needs.

12.2 Data Quality and Compatibility Assurance:

Effective AI integration relies on the quality and compatibility of data. This section explores strategies for ensuring data quality, addressing compatibility issues, and establishing robust data governance practices. From data validation to implementing standardized formats, the focus is on creating a reliable data foundation for AI algorithms.

12.3 Addressing Organizational Resistance:

Overcoming resistance within an organization is often a critical aspect of successful integration. The chapter delves into change management strategies, communication plans, and the importance of involving stakeholders early in the process to build acceptance and enthusiasm for AI technologies.

12.4 Aligning AI with Existing Infrastructure:

Harmonizing AI with existing control systems poses challenges that require strategic solutions. This section explores approaches such as gradual integration, adapting AI algorithms to complement current systems, and conducting thorough compatibility tests. The aim is to create a cohesive ecosystem where AI seamlessly complements established infrastructure.

12.5 Mitigating Cybersecurity Concerns:

With the integration of AI, cybersecurity becomes a paramount concern. The chapter discusses robust cybersecurity measures, encryption protocols, and continuous monitoring practices to safeguard against potential cyber threats. Emphasizing the importance of a proactive cybersecurity stance, organizations can ensure the integrity of AI-powered turbine systems.

12.6 Scalability and Future-Proofing:

Ensuring the scalability and future-proofing of integrated systems is a crucial consideration. This section explores modular design principles, flexible architectures, and selecting AI solutions that can adapt to evolving technological landscapes. Scalability ensures that integrated systems can accommodate growth and emerging technologies.

12.7 Continuous Monitoring and Evaluation:

Sustained success post-integration relies on continuous monitoring and evaluation. The chapter underscores the significance of ongoing assessments, feedback loops, and periodic evaluations. This iterative process ensures that AI systems remain aligned with operational objectives and can be adjusted in response to changing requirements.

12.8 Best Practices for Seamless Integration:

The chapter concludes by consolidating best practices distilled from successful AI integration endeavors. From fostering a culture of innovation and transparency to establishing cross-functional collaboration, these best practices serve as a guide for organizations aiming not just for successful integration but also for the ongoing optimization of AI-powered turbine operations.

Chapter 12 equips readers with practical insights and strategies to navigate the complexities of AI integration, emphasizing the importance of addressing challenges and implementing best practices. As we progress through the subsequent chapters, the focus on integration challenges and solutions remains integral, shaping a narrative that empowers organizations to embrace AI seamlessly in their turbine operations.

CHAPTER THIRTEEN

Ethical Considerations in AI-Driven Operations

In this crucial chapter of "The AI Turbine Handbook," we explore the ethical dimensions of AI-driven operations in power generation. As AI becomes increasingly intertwined with critical infrastructure, it is imperative to ensure responsible and ethical usage. This chapter delves into the ethical considerations, addresses concerns, and outlines strategies to build trust in AI applications within turbine operations.

13.1 Ethical Frameworks for AI Integration:

The chapter commences by establishing the ethical foundations for AI integration in turbine operations. It explores existing ethical frameworks, such as fairness, transparency, accountability, and privacy, which should guide the development and deployment of AI technologies in the power generation sector.

13.2 Fairness in AI Decision-Making:

Ensuring fairness in AI algorithms is a serious consideration. This section discusses the challenges associated with biases in AI models and strategies for mitigating them. From diverse dataset curation to regular audits, the focus is on cultivating fairness to prevent discriminatory outcomes in turbine operations.

13.3 Transparency and Explainability:

Transparency and explainability are pivotal for building trust in AI systems. The chapter delves into the importance of making AI decision-making processes understandable to stakeholders. Strategies include adopting transparent algorithms, providing explanations for AI-driven decisions, and fostering a culture of openness in turbine operations.

13.4 Accountability in AI-Enhanced Operations:

Assigning accountability is a key ethical consideration. This section explores the allocation of responsibility for AI decisions, emphasizing the need for clear lines of accountability. Strategies include defining roles and responsibilities, establishing oversight mechanisms, and implementing protocols for addressing unforeseen consequences.

13.5 Privacy Protection in AI Applications:

Protecting privacy is paramount, especially when dealing with sensitive operational data. The chapter addresses privacy concerns related to AI integration and outlines strategies for data anonymization, secure data storage, and compliance with privacy regulations to safeguard individual and organizational privacy.

13.6 Ethical Considerations in Human-AI Collaboration:

As AI collaborates with human operators, ethical considerations come to the forefront. This section explores the dynamics of human-AI collaboration, emphasizing the importance of mutual respect, clear communication, and defining boundaries to ensure ethical practices in turbine operations.

13.7 Addressing Bias and Discrimination:

Bias and discrimination can inadvertently be embedded in AI models. The chapter discusses strategies for identifying and mitigating biases, including ongoing monitoring, diverse stakeholder involvement, and continuous improvement to foster fairness and equality.

13.8 Building Trust Through Ethical Practices:

The chapter concludes by elucidating how ethical practices are foundational for building trust in AI-driven operations. It emphasizes the importance of communication, transparency, and adherence to ethical principles in creating a trustworthy environment around AI integration within turbine operations.

Chapter 13 navigates the complex terrain of ethical considerations in AI-driven turbine operations. By adopting responsible practices and addressing concerns proactively, organizations can not only ensure the ethical deployment of AI technologies but also build trust among stakeholders. As we progress through the subsequent chapters, the ethical considerations in AI applications continue to play a pivotal role, shaping a future where AI operates with integrity and responsibility in power generation.

CONCLUSION

Shaping the Future of AI in Turbine Operations

In concluding "The AI Turbine Handbook," let's recap key takeaways and cast a forward gaze into the future landscape of AI in turbine operations.

Summary of Key Takeaways:

AI Fundamentals: The journey began with fundamentals, understanding AI's role in power generation, emphasizing its transformative impact on efficiency, maintenance, and decision-making.

Integration Challenges: We navigated through the challenges of integrating AI, addressing issues like data compatibility, organizational resistance, and the imperative alignment of AI with existing control systems.

Ethical Considerations: The ethical dimensions of AI integration were explored, emphasizing fairness, transparency, accountability, and privacy as foundational pillars. Human-AI collaboration and addressing biases emerged as critical aspects of ethical AI practices.

Emerging Technologies: The horizon of emerging technologies showcased innovations in materials, quantum computing, the Internet of Things (IoT), edge computing, and explainable AI, contributing to the continual evolution of turbine operations.

Case Studies: Real-world case studies illuminated the tangible benefits of AI in power generation, ranging from predictive maintenance and dynamic control systems to cybersecurity resilience and economic impacts.

Regulatory Compliance: The chapter on regulatory compliance underscored the importance of aligning AI practices with industry standards, ensuring a harmonious integration within the regulatory landscape.

Future Trends: Exploring future trends revealed emerging technologies such as quantum computing, IoT, edge computing, and sustainable AI applications, shaping a future where turbines operate with increased efficiency, sustainability, and autonomy.

Conclusion: Ethical considerations emerged as a crucial aspect, emphasizing responsible AI usage, addressing concerns, and building trust in AI-driven operations.

Looking Ahead: The Future Landscape of AI in Turbine Operations:

As we peer into the future, the integration of AI into turbine operations is poised for continued innovation and growth. The landscape is characterized by:

Advanced Autonomy: AI-driven turbines will exhibit advanced autonomy in operations and maintenance, optimizing performance with minimal human intervention.

Sustainability Integration: AI will play a pivotal role in integrating sustainable practices, optimizing energy efficiency, and dynamically adjusting operations based on renewable energy availability.

Human-AI Synergy: Human-AI collaboration will evolve, fostering a synergistic partnership where AI augments human capabilities, leading to more efficient decision-making and troubleshooting.

Continual Ethical Evolution: Ethical considerations will remain at the forefront, with ongoing developments in fairness, transparency, and accountability to ensure the responsible deployment of AI in turbine operations.

Enhanced Cybersecurity Measures: As AI becomes more integral, cybersecurity measures will evolve to safeguard against emerging threats, ensuring the secure and reliable operation of AI-driven turbine systems.

Data-Driven Decision-Making: AI will continue to refine data-driven decision-making, with advancements in predictive analytics, machine learning applications, and real-time monitoring shaping a future where turbines are optimized based on precise insights.

"The AI Turbine Handbook" concludes with the anticipation of a future where AI not only optimizes turbine operations but does so with ethical integrity, sustainability, and a harmonious integration within the broader energy landscape. As the journey continues, the collaboration between human ingenuity and AI-driven innovation will define the path toward a more efficient, resilient, and sustainable future in power generation.